EXTREME SPORTS EVENTS

4 DESERTS ULTRAMARATHON SERIES

LUKE HANLON

SportsZone
An Imprint of Abdo Publishing
abdobooks.com

abdobooks.com

Published by Abdo Publishing, a division of ABDO, PO Box 398166, Minneapolis, Minnesota 55439. Copyright © 2024 by Abdo Consulting Group, Inc. International copyrights reserved in all countries. No part of this book may be reproduced in any form without written permission from the publisher. SportsZone™ is a trademark and logo of Abdo Publishing.

Printed in the United States of America, North Mankato, Minnesota.
102023
012024

Cover Photo: Jean-Philippe Ksiazek/AFP/Getty Images
Interior Photos: Thiago Diz/RacingThePlanet Limited, 4–5, 6, 10–11, 12, 15, 17, 18, 20, 22–23, 25, 26–27, 29; Red Line Editorial, 9

Editors: Charlie Beattie and Steph Giedd
Series Designer: Cynthia Della-Rovere

Library of Congress Control Number: 2023939470

Publisher's Cataloging-in-Publication Data

Names: Hanlon, Luke, author.
Title: 4 Deserts Ultramarathon Series / by Luke Hanlon
Other Title: Four Deserts Ultramarathon Series
Description: Minneapolis, Minnesota: Abdo Publishing, 2024 | Series: Extreme sports events | Includes online resources and index.
Identifiers: ISBN 9781098292355 (lib. bdg.) | ISBN 9798384910299 (ebook)
Subjects: LCSH: Extreme sports--Juvenile literature. | Action sports (Extreme sports)--Juvenile literature. | Ultra-marathon running--Juvenile literature. | Running races--Juvenile literature. | Deserts--Juvenile literature.
Classification: DDC 796.046--dc23

TABLE OF CONTENTS

CHAPTER 1
The Long March 4

CHAPTER 2
Ready for Anything.............. 10

CHAPTER 3
Hot and Cold 16

CHAPTER 4
Grand Slam 22

Glossary............................. 30
More Information 31
Online Resources................ 31
Index 32
About the Author............... 32

CHAPTER 1

THE LONG MARCH

While hiking through the Namib Desert, Elise Zender came across a gravestone. For the racer, it felt like a fitting image. The extreme heat and lack of wind was making Zender feel faint. She thought she would need her own gravestone at any moment. Although she didn't know it at the time, she was dealing with an infection caused by parasites that were eating away at her red blood cells. She felt the urge to throw up. But there was nothing in her stomach to get rid of.

Zender was competing in the Namib Race in 2022, which is part of the 4 Deserts Ultramarathon Series. She was on the fourth day of a seven-day race that covered 155 miles (250 km) in Namibia, a country in southwest

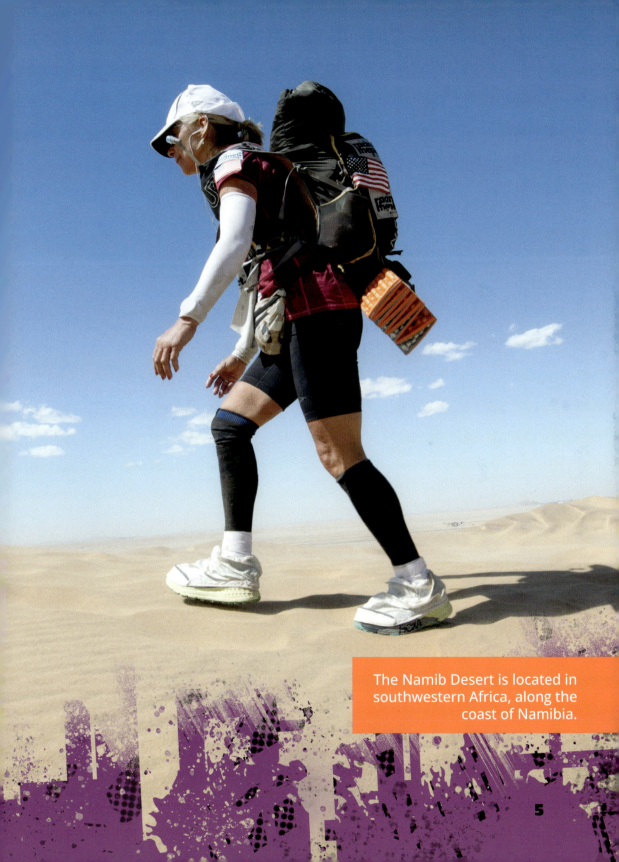

The Namib Desert is located in southwestern Africa, along the coast of Namibia.

Running on rocks and sand, such as during the Namib Race, can be challenging and may cause injuries.

Africa. Her fatigue and dehydration had slowed her pace to a crawl. While she was suffering, she kept reminding herself that pain is just temporary. Shortly after she reached a checkpoint, a volunteer asked her if she wanted to drop out of the race. But thinking about the disappointment of quitting gave her the motivation she needed to keep going.

She finished the fourth day in one piece. However, the fifth day was the Long March. Zender woke up 30 minutes before she was scheduled to start a 50-mile (80-km) hike. She was still dealing with nausea and severe foot pain from the days of hiking. But Zender slowly worked her way through the hike. Despite the long distance, this was her favorite day of the race. One of the fields she hiked through was covered in rose quartz. The beauty of the 4 Deserts races provides some distraction from the pain the athletes endure.

The hike took so long that Zender had to travel alone across the desert at night. Her headlamp gave out, and she could hear the screams of hyenas in the distance. Yet she felt calm walking through the darkness. After arriving at camp at 2 a.m., Zender was able to rest her blistered feet. She was exhausted, but she was excited to be close to the finish line.

MORE THAN ONE RACE

As the name suggests, the 4 Deserts Ultramarathon Series is made up of four long races that take place in four different deserts. Each race is 155 miles (250 km) long and occurs over the course of seven days. The four races take place on four different continents: Africa, Antarctica, Asia, and South America.

Mary Gadams founded the series in 2002. As an ultramarathoner herself, she wanted to come up with a global race. The idea was to combine her favorite parts of the races in which she had previously competed. Gadams also wanted competitors to experience four different settings that each provided their own set of challenges. That's how the 4 Deserts races ended up taking place in some of the most extreme weather conditions in the world.

The first race of the year is the Namib Race, which takes place in April in Namibia. Athletes race through the oldest desert in the world, dealing with hot temperatures. In June athletes can travel to Mongolia in Asia to compete in the Gobi March. This race is scenic and includes sections through old forests. The next race is the Atacama Crossing in September. This race takes place in Chile, a country in western South America. The Atacama is considered the driest place on Earth. It's also rocky and features many salt flats. The final race is The Last Desert in Antarctica. This race is held every two years. Every other November, competitors travel to Antarctica to complete the race in the freezing cold.

Athletes can compete in any of the individual races or attempt all four in a given year. Of the four races,

4 DESERTS ULTRAMARATHON SERIES

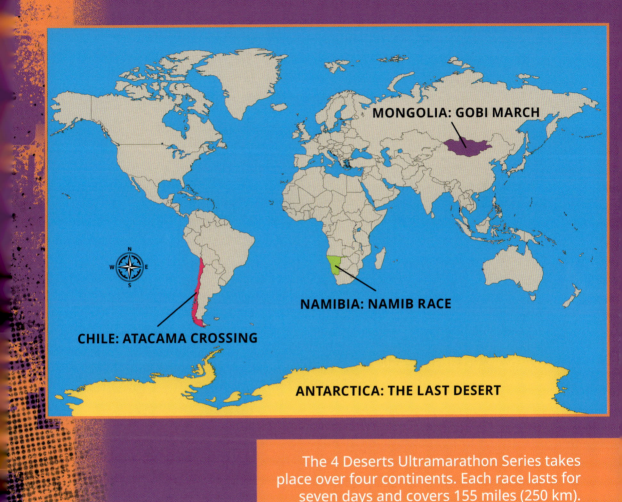

The 4 Deserts Ultramarathon Series takes place over four continents. Each race lasts for seven days and covers 155 miles (250 km).

The Last Desert is the only one with a qualifier. Athletes must complete at least two races in the 4 Deserts series before they can compete in The Last Desert. That way the organizers know that those athletes are up for the challenge of hiking across the coldest desert on the planet.

CHAPTER 2

READY FOR ANYTHING

To make sure participants are ready for the 4 Deserts Ultramarathon Series, the organizers of the race have specific training plans on their website. There are plans for beginning, intermediate, and advanced athletes. If followed correctly, these plans can help anyone complete an ultramarathon. That includes athletes who compete in them regularly and those who have no experience running long distances.

While the intensity and distances of workouts vary by each level, all three follow the same 24-week structure. The schedule is broken into six periods of four weeks each. Each one focuses on preparing for a different part of the race. This includes things like

Some runners compete with trekking poles to help with the different types of terrain they will encounter.

Racers must be prepared to carry their own food and supplies. Competitors are only provided with drinking water and a tent to sleep in each night.

learning how to recover properly, hiking with heavy weight in a backpack, and training early in the morning.

These workouts are not just running or hiking, however. Though that is what competitors will have to do in any of the 4 Deserts races, the workout plans include non-load-bearing exercises such as cycling, swimming, or yoga. The idea is not to overwork an athlete's body. Workouts get longer as the race gets closer. The peak workout comes two weeks before the event. The suggestion for beginners is a four-hour hike with a 22-pound (10-kg) pack. The weight of the pack is the same for advanced athletes. But more advanced competitors are expected to add a two-hour jog to the end of a four-hour hike.

A HEAVY LOAD

Each race in the 4 Deserts presents its own issues. One consistent challenge in all four races is that competitors must carry all their equipment with them. While training, hiking with a weighted pack is important because that's exactly what competitors must do during a 4 Deserts race. Given all the required food and equipment athletes must carry, a pack can weigh close to 30 pounds (14 kg).

There is a mandatory set of items a competitor must have to even start the race. Those items are a backpack, a sleeping bag, shoes, a headlamp, a red flashing light, and

GAITERS

Gaiters are an important piece of equipment for the 4 Deserts. These are a piece of clothing worn over shoes and the bottom of pants to protect runners from getting debris in their shoes. They are perfect for running through sand and can keep feet dry when traveling through streams, creeks, or snow.

a compass. They also need food and drinks containing the proper amounts of calories and electrolytes. A minimum of 2,000 calories per day is needed. That means 14,000 calories must be stored in an athlete's backpack and carried during the race with all their other equipment.

That rule is in place to make sure athletes stay nourished while they're competing. It also forces athletes to consider the weight of the food they bring with them. While training for the race, it is important for athletes to try different energy gels or bars, which can provide roughly 100 calories per pack. Once athletes are done with the day's course, freeze-dried foods can provide protein to help athletes recover from a long day of exercise.

Knowing how to stay hydrated also helps athletes remain in the race. Water is one of the only things provided to athletes that they do not have to carry themselves. But drinking just water is not enough to avoid becoming dehydrated in the desert. That is why athletes carry drinks with a lot of electrolytes while they compete. Those drinks help the body replenish what has been lost through sweat better than water does. Learning how much to eat or drink while competing is all a part of the training process. And it can be the difference between finishing the race or not.

Staying hydrated is crucial in order to avoid dehydration, which can lead to other health issues and injuries.

HOT AND COLD

People who have competed in the Namib Race have described the setting as beautiful. Despite its pretty views, the Namib Desert provides plenty of challenges to the athletes who race through it. One of the biggest is dealing with all the sand. Being surrounded by sand is not unusual in a desert. But the gusting winds in Namibia toss the sand all over. It can significantly slow competitors down. The swirling sand can also end up in annoying places like an athlete's shoes or backpack. It can sometimes end up in the athletes themselves. Beth Whitman competed in the Namib Race in 2021. She said it took her multiple days after the race to fully clean the sand grains out of her ears.

For many competitors, the scenic views make the race worth the challenge.

Racers are able to rest, hydrate, and connect with other competitors at the end of each race day.

In the Gobi March, the setting and terrain change dramatically throughout the race. The early stages take place across mountain ranges that can reach 9,500 feet (2,900 m) above sea level. That altitude also brings freezing temperatures and possible hailstorms that athletes must be prepared to deal with.

If that isn't difficult enough, the Long March of this race takes place in the Gobi Desert. Competitors must travel 50 miles (80 km) through the desert on days four and five of the race. During that hike, temperatures can reach as high as 124 degrees Fahrenheit (51°C). To support the athletes, water is provided at checkpoints every six miles (10 km). But competitor Michael Sheesley didn't find the liquids to be very refreshing, because the beverages aren't chilled. When he did the Gobi March in 2016, he was given soda and water to beat the heat. He said taking in the warm liquids in the Gobi was "like drinking hot tea on the beach . . . with no ocean in sight."

THE ATACAMA FLATS

Getting hot water is still better than no water. One of the stages of the Atacama Crossing goes through a field of salt flats. The terrain is covered in sharp shards of salt that don't break when they're stepped on. Because of the uneven nature of the ground, it is nearly impossible for support vehicles to drive on this surface, so athletes try to rely on their own supplies to stay hydrated.

The salt flats are also dangerous for the competitors to walk on. Sarah Oppermann competed in the Atacama Crossing in 2019. She said she witnessed other

MEDICAL COCA-COLA

Soda is not a regular part of most ultramarathoners' diets. However, the sugar rush provided by soda can help athletes get through a day during the 4 Deserts. Volunteers offer Coca-Cola at certain checkpoints to provide a boost to racers.

Racers in The Last Desert use bright markers to guide them through the all-white, snowy conditions.

athletes twisting their ankles while hiking through the field. Some even came away with stress fractures in their legs due to the tough terrain.

THE FROZEN RACE

The Last Desert takes place during the summer in Antarctica. But the temperatures are still below freezing. And instead of walking through sand, athletes hike through snow and ice during The Last Desert. When Brendan Funk completed The Last Desert in 2016, he did so in extreme pain. The cold terrain caused injuries in his lower back and his legs. That put more strain on his mind, as he worked to convince himself that finishing the brutally cold course was worth it.

The setup of the race is slightly different as well. The runners live on a boat. Each day, the boat takes the competitors to a different Antarctic island. There, athletes complete repeated loops of each course to get to the required distance. Each loop in The Last Desert is shorter than a stage in one of the other three races. But athletes still must cover 155 miles (250 km) to complete the race. That means they hike each loop multiple times, for up to 15 hours each day.

CHAPTER 4

GRAND SLAM

It is not cheap to compete in any of the 4 Deserts races. Entry into the Atacama, Gobi, or Namib costs approximately $4,000. If someone finishes two of those races and wants to compete in The Last Desert, that'll cost another $13,900. And there is no cash prize for winning or finishing the race.

While none of the competitors can win any money, a lot of them compete to raise money for others. The organizers of the 4 Deserts encourage athletes to compete for a specific charity to which people can donate. This gives athletes a bigger purpose than just racing for their own satisfaction.

Anne-Marie Flammersfeld completed every 4 Deserts race in 2012. She competed to raise money for her charity called Paulchen

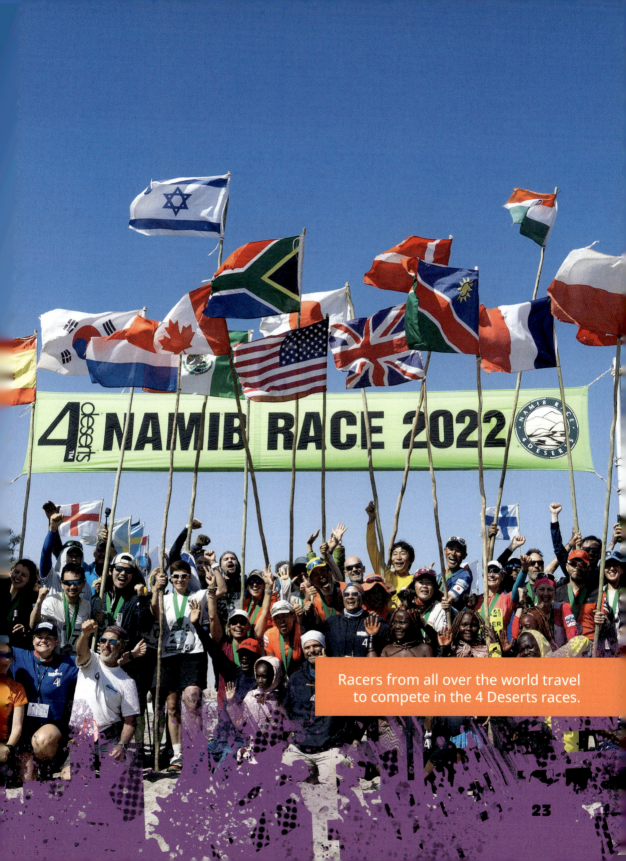
Racers from all over the world travel to compete in the 4 Deserts races.

Esperanza, which supports children in poverty. Four years later, Jax Mariash Mustafa completed all of the 4 Deserts races to raise money for the LymeLight Foundation. That charity provides medical assistance to children suffering from Lyme disease. Since the series began in 2002, 4 Deserts has supported dozens of charities. And its competitors have helped raise millions of dollars for people around the world.

On top of the personal satisfaction that comes with completing a 4 Deserts race, the athletes can compete for trophies. None is more prestigious than the 4 Deserts World Champion. That goes to the man and woman who have the highest combined ranking in each of the 4 Desert races across their ultramarathon careers.

SMILE INTERNATIONAL

The charity that 4 Deserts has supported the most since the series began is Operation Smile International. It helps children receive surgeries to address cleft conditions such as a cleft lip or cleft palate. These are gaps in the mouth that can cause difficulty with eating and speaking. Since 2003 the 4 Deserts series has raised more than $750,000 for the charity.

BEYOND GLORY

Athletes don't have to win races to be recognized, however. Any athlete who completes all four races joins the 4 Deserts Club.

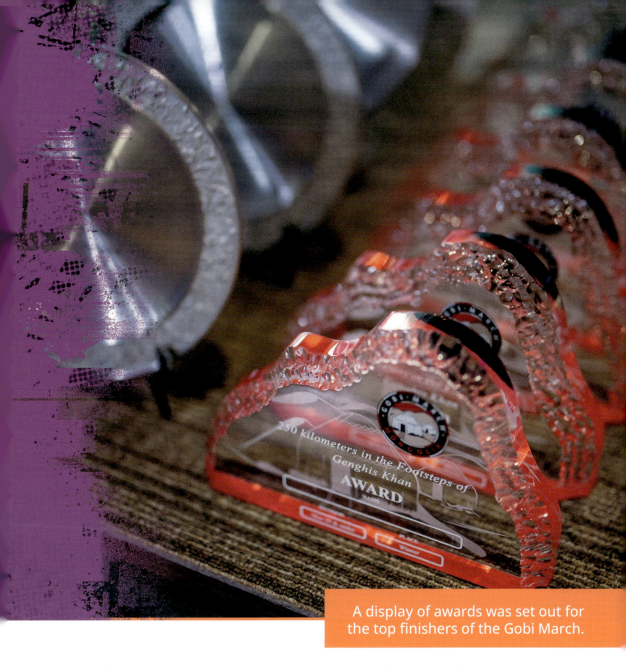

A display of awards was set out for the top finishers of the Gobi March.

There is an even more exclusive club called the 4 Deserts Grand Slam. To gain access to that club, athletes must complete all four races in the same year. Los Angeles native Dean Karnazes is one of the most accomplished endurance

athletes in the world. Known as the "Ultramarathon Man," Karnazes was the first person ever to complete the 4 Deserts Grand Slam, doing so in 2008. Since he completed it, more than 80 other athletes have endured all four races in a single year.

Runners who finish one of the races receive a finisher's medal. But for many, finishing the race is reward enough.

The 4 Deserts has also seen athletes of all ages compete in its races. When Brendan Funk completed The Last Desert in 2016, he was 21. That made him the youngest person to complete the 4 Deserts Grand Slam. Three years later, Bill Mitchell completed the Atacama

Crossing at 75. That made him the oldest person ever to finish a 4 Deserts race.

AFTER THE FINISH

Once any athlete has completed a race, it's time to recover. It usually takes competitors five to seven days for their bodies to get back to normal. Some go back to their regular lives at that point. However, many others start training for the next race in the series.

When Michael Sheesley competed in the Gobi March in 2016, a rest day was set aside for racers on the sixth day of competition. Instead of hiking, they could relax at a camp set up for the racers.

During this break from racing, Sheesley struck up a conversation with fellow competitor Michael Thompson. The pair talked about how special it was to be doing something that most human beings wouldn't even try, let alone finish. They also decided that the challenge of the Gobi race had helped make them better people.

The next day, Sheesley hiked the final 6.2 miles (10 km) to the finish. His race was over. Sheesley was injured and sleep deprived. But he couldn't wait to compete in a 4 Deserts race again.

Competitors cross paths with a Gentoo penguin during The Last Desert.

GLOSSARY

calorie
A unit of measure of energy in food.

charity
An organization that exists to help certain people or groups.

debris
Broken pieces left over after something has been destroyed.

dehydration
A condition in which the body does not have enough water.

electrolytes
Essential minerals that are vital to the human body.

exclusive
Not available to everyone.

fatigue
Extreme tiredness.

Lyme disease
An illness that is transferred by ticks and can lead to other serious health problems.

parasite
Something that lives in or on another creature and causes harm to that creature.

rose quartz
Rocks that are a clear shade of pink.

salt flat
An area of land covered with a layer of salt.

stress fracture
A broken bone that is caused by repeated use.

terrain
The physical qualities of the land within a region.

MORE INFORMATION

BOOKS

Feng, Kelly. *Ultra-Trail du Mont-Blanc.* Minneapolis, MN: Abdo Publishing, 2024.

Hewson, Anthony K. *Arrowhead 135.* Minneapolis, MN: Abdo Publishing, 2024.

Hewson, Anthony K. *Badwater 135.* Minneapolis, MN: Abdo Publishing, 2024.

ONLINE RESOURCES

To learn more about the 4 Deserts Ultramarathon Series, please visit **abdobooklinks.com** or scan this QR code. These links are routinely monitored and updated to provide the most current information available.

INDEX

Antarctica, 8, 21
Atacama Crossing, 8, 19, 22, 27–28

Chile, 8

Flammersfeld, Anne-Marie, 22
4 Deserts Club, 24
4 Deserts Grand Slam, 25–27
4 Deserts World Champion, 24
Funk, Brendan, 21, 27

Gadams, Mary, 8
Gobi Desert, 18–19
Gobi March, 8, 18–19, 22, 28

Karnazes, Dean, 25–26

Last Desert, The, 8–9, 21, 22, 27
Long March, the, 7, 18
LymeLight Foundation, 24

Mitchell, Bill, 27
Mongolia, 8
Mustafa, Jax Mariash, 24

Namib Desert, 4, 16
Namib Race, 4, 8, 16, 22
Namibia, 4, 8, 16

Operation Smile International, 24
Oppermann, Sarah, 19

Paulchen Esperanza, 22–24

Sheesley, Michael, 19, 28

Thompson, Michael, 28

Whitman, Beth, 16

Zender, Elise, 4, 7

ABOUT THE AUTHOR

Luke Hanlon is a sportswriter and editor based in Minneapolis.